W9-ABC-164

A.R. 3.9

Pts. 0.5

The SPICE Alphabet Book

herbs, spices, and other natural flavors

by Jerry Pallotta

illustrated by Leslie Evans

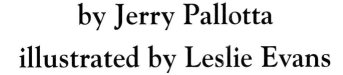

ini Charlesbridge

Published by
Charlesbridge Publishing
85 Main Street, Watertown, MA 02172-4411
(617) 926-0329

Printed in the United States of America
(sc) 10 9 8 7 6 5 4 3 2 1
(hc) 10 9 8 7 6 5 4 3 2 1

Printed on Recycled Paper.

Library of Congress Cataloging-in-Publication Data
Pallotta, Jerry.
    The spice alphabet book: herbs, spices, and other
natural flavors / by Jerry Pallotta; illustrated by Leslie
Evans.
        p.   cm.
    ISBN 0-88106-899-3 (library reinforced)
    ISBN 0-88106-898-5 (hardcover)
    ISBN 0-88106-897-7 (softcover)
    1. Spices—Juvenile literature. 2. Herbs—
Juvenile literature. 3. English language—Alphabet—
Juvenile literature. [1. Spices. 2. Herbs. 3. Alphabet.]
I. Evans, Leslie. II. Title.
TX406.P27 1994
641.6'383 — dc20
                                        94-5178
                                          CIP
                                          AC

Books by Jerry Pallotta:
  The Icky Bug Alphabet Book
  The Icky Bug Counting Book
  The Bird Alphabet Book
  The Ocean Alphabet Book
  The Flower Alphabet Book
  The Yucky Reptile Alphabet Book
  The Frog Alphabet Book
  The Furry Alphabet Book
  The Dinosaur Alphabet Book
  The Underwater Alphabet Book
  The Victory Garden Vegetable Alphabet Book
  The Extinct Alphabet Book
  The Desert Alphabet Book
  The Spice Alphabet Book
  Going Lobstering
  Cuenta los insectos (The Icky Bug Counting Book)
  The Make Your Own Alphabet Book

A zillion thanks to
Dr. Arthur "Sonny" Pallotta,
biochemist, toxicologist, scientist,
uncle, and above all, friend.

These illustrations are dedicated in memory
of my wonderful mother, Shirley Mays Evans.

Many thanks to Pamela Ryan and Rosalie Davis
for their help in the preparation of this book.

Aa

A is for Anise. Anise is a spice that comes from a seed and tastes like licorice. *What is a spice?*

A spice is the section of a plant that has the flavor. The spice flavor could be from the bark, the stem, the flower, the bean, the nut, the oil, the sap, the seed, the leaf, or the root of a plant.

anise drops

jelly beans

THAYERS HONEY & ANISE COUGH SYRUP WITH BEE PROPOLIS 4 FL. OZ.

Anise seeds .75 ¼ lb

ANIS PASTILLES NET WT 1¾ OZ

anise oil ½ FL. OZ.

FRESH BASIL
1 50 EXTRA FANCY
BUNCH

basil

GINGER 99¢ POUND

FRESH CILANTRO 2 FOR 1 50

DILL 2 FOR 1 50

WATERCRESS 2 FOR 1 50

TOMATOES 79¢ POUND

Bb

B is for Basil. Basil is an herb. If you go to market, walk near the fresh Basil and take a good whiff. It smells wonderful. *What is an herb?*

An herb is an edible green leaf that is used to season foods.

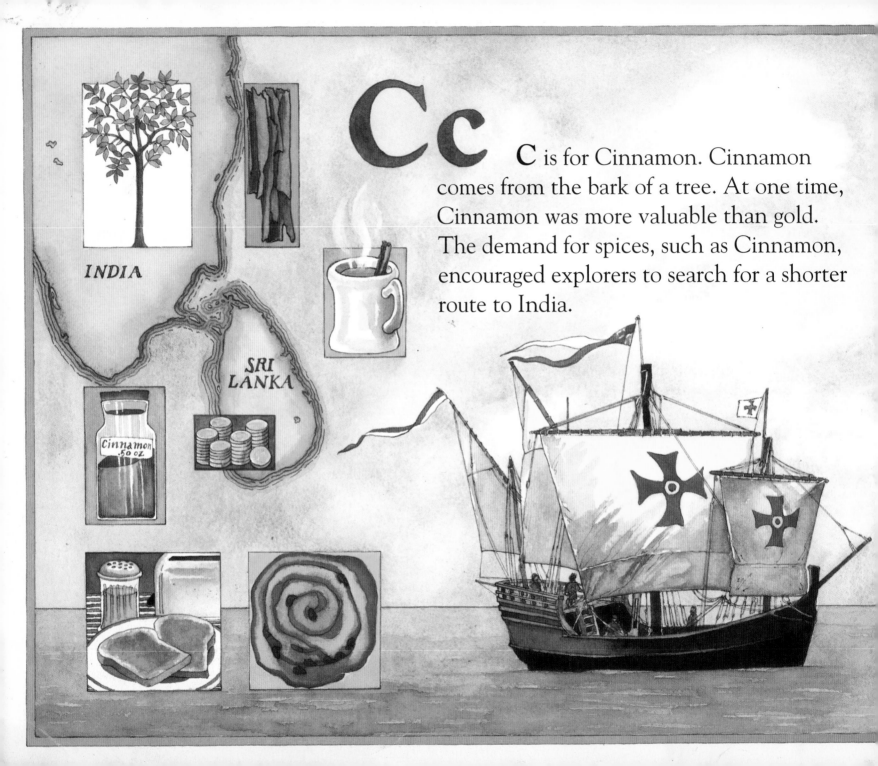

Cc

C is for Cinnamon. Cinnamon comes from the bark of a tree. At one time, Cinnamon was more valuable than gold. The demand for spices, such as Cinnamon, encouraged explorers to search for a shorter route to India.

INDIA

SRI LANKA

Cinnamon
.50 OZ.

Dd

D is for Dill. Whenever you say the word Dill, people immediately think of pickles. Dill peanut butter, Dill ice cream, and Dill milk do not sound right. Dill pickles sounds perfect!

dill weed
.90 oz

Ee

E is for Eucalyptus. When you had a cold, maybe someone rubbed your chest with Eucalyptus salve or gave you a Eucalyptus cough drop. Or, maybe you took a bath that steamed up the room with the smell of Eucalyptus.

F is for Fennel. Fennel is an herb and a spice. All parts of the plant are edible. You can eat the fresh or dried green leaves. You can use the seeds for baking. You can also eat the stalk and bulb like a piece of celery.

Gg

G is for Garlic. Garlic has a powerful flavor! If you eat a lot of Garlic on Monday, someone might still smell it on your breath on Tuesday or even Wednesday. But, don't worry. Eating Garlic is good for you.

WELCOME TO GILROY GARLIC CAPITAL OF THE WORLD

Gg

G is also for Ginger. The Ginger flavor comes from a root. It has a taste that is hard to describe. If you bite into raw Ginger, it seems to bite back.

Have you ever made a gingerbread house?

Molasses Spice Crisps   Grandma
2½ cups sifted flour
2 tsp each of ginger, cloves, cinnamon and baking soda
Sift flour once, measure and add soda + spices.
    Sift together 3 times.
Cream ¾ cup shortening, add 1 cup sugar
    gradually and cream together.
Add 1 egg unbeaten - beat well. Then add
4 Tbsp molasses, flour and mix thoroughly.
Chill dough - roll in balls and dip in sugar.
Place on greased cookie sheet.
Bake 15 to 20 minutes at 350°.

Ginger
.50-oz

Thou shalt not steal

Hh

H is for Herb Garden. If you want to grow an Herb Garden, you do not need much room. You can grow one in a window box, between the rungs of a ladder, or even in an old boat. Your Herb Garden might attract a hummingbird and a few butterflies.

HYSSOP

herb

Shirley Seeds

Habanero
PEPPER

HOT STUFF
MUÑOZ SEEDS

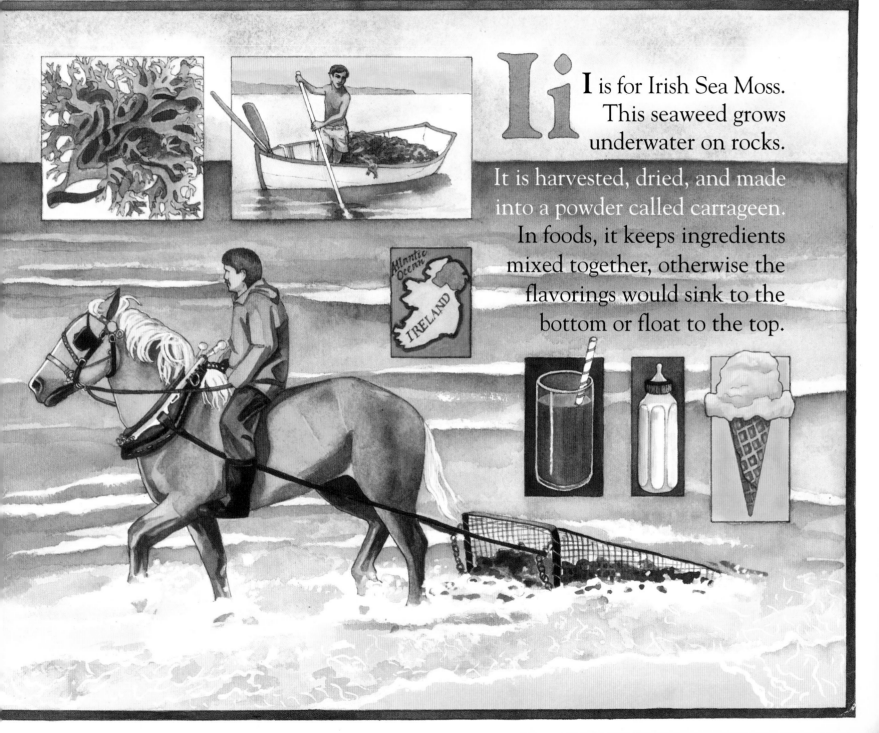

I is for Irish Sea Moss. This seaweed grows underwater on rocks.

It is harvested, dried, and made into a powder called carrageen. In foods, it keeps ingredients mixed together, otherwise the flavorings would sink to the bottom or float to the top.

Jj

It's time for a COFFEE BREAK!

J is for Java. Java is another name for coffee. Java is also an island in Indonesia where coffee is grown. Think of all the vocabulary that includes the word coffee, such as coffee table, coffee cake, coffee pot, and coffee break!

OCIA certified
ORGANIC
Pluma
Coixtepec
STRICTLY HIGH GROWN
OAXACA
Mexico

CAFÉ DO BRASIL
/23 02/0
KENYA A
LOT G
BREM

YS
YAUCO SELECTO
HIGH MOUNTAIN GROWN

SHIPPED BY: YAUCO SELECTO, S.E.
NET WEIGHT 100 LBS.(45.36KG.)
PREMIUM COFFEE GROWN IN PUERTO RICO
SIZE: A

★ GRACIAS A LOS CORSOS

SAN FRANCISCO
COFFEE BEANS
PRODUCE OF JAVA
INDONESIA
1-200

MATARI
O. YEMEN

Coca-Cola ®

Coca-Cola

TRADE MARK REGISTERED
BOTTLE PAT D DEC. 25. 1923

Mediterranean Sea

WEST AFRICA

Tropical Rain Forest

Atlantic Ocean

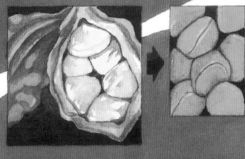

Kk

K is for Kola.
Kola nuts are the seeds from the Kola tree that grows in tropical Africa. One of the most popular drinks in the world is a soda flavored with an extract made from Kola nuts.

L is for Lavender. If we were going to eat or drink all of the great tasting things in this book, it would be a good idea to wash our hands first. Lavender is a fragrance used in making soap.

CAN THESE GUYS CUT THE MUSTARD?

CITGO

Dijon •
FRANCE

Please SOX CUBS R H E INN pass
1

SOX CUBS 1 2 3 4 5 6 7 8 9 10 R H E

Mustard Seed

Mm

M is for Mustard. People often associate tastes and smells with places they have been. The smell of Mustard can bring back the memory of a home run, with the bases loaded, in the bottom of the ninth inning. This spice can take you out to the ball game!

Mm

M is also for Maple. This flavor comes from the sap of certain Maple trees. When it is tapped, the sap is very watery. After it is boiled, it thickens and becomes delicious Maple syrup.

N is for Nutmeg. This spice comes from a hard nut that is grated into powder. Nutmeg's unique flavor can add that extra special zing to desserts that already taste wonderful. If you do not like Nutmeg, you must be nuts!

whole nutmeg

mace

Oo

O is for Oregano. Oregano is often used to flavor tomato sauce. Tomato sauce is used on top of spaghetti and pizza. The person who wrote this book loves pizza. Do you?

oros ganos

oregano
.50 oz

Pp

P is for Pepper. Just thinking about this page . . . Ah ah ah . . . can make you ah ah ah ah . . . Sneeze! AH CHOO! It wouldn't be fair to mention pepper without mentioning salt.

Salt is a flavor, but it does not come from a plant. Salt is a mineral.

SUPER HOT CHILI

pepper-corns

cayenne .50 oz

Qq

Q is for Quinine. Quinine comes from the bark of a cinchona tree. It gives a bitter flavoring to the carbonated drink called tonic water. It is also a medicine. During the construction of the Panama Canal, many workers got sick from malaria and were treated with Quinine.

parsley sage rosemary thyme

Rr

R is for Rosemary. This herb feels and smells like pine needles. Rosemary has always been known as the herb of remembrance. It is nice to send a sprig of Rosemary to a person you love.

rosemary leaves

Ss S is for Spearmint.

Spearmint and peppermint are aromatic herbs that are used to flavor candy, gum, and toothpaste. It is fun to eat candy, but don't forget to brush your teeth.

T should be for tea, but it's not.

T is for Tarragon. Tarragon is an herb that is popular in gourmet kitchens. Great chefs around the world have been cooking with it for hundreds of years.

Uu

U is for Uva-ursi.
Uva-ursi is also called bearberry.
People do not usually eat Uva-ursi.
Bears love to eat it, but bears
cannot read this book.

V v

V is for Vanilla. Vanilla is the most popular ice cream flavor in the world. The Vanilla bean comes from the pod of an orchid flower. This flavor was discovered in the tropical rain forest.

Thank you, rain forest.

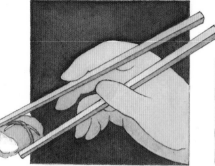

Ww

W is for Wasabi. The bright green stuff on your plate at a sushi restaurant is a hot spice that comes from the root of the Wasabi plant. If you try Wasabi, only take a teeny-weeny taste.

Xx

When the people of Central and South America discovered it, they thought it was a gift from the gods. Today, people worldwide still consider it to be the ultimate flavor.

X is for Xocoatl. Xocoatl is the Aztec word for chocolate.

Yy

Here is the tea page!

Y is for Yaupon. Many years ago, when people could not afford to buy tea, they brewed their own from the leaves of the Yaupon holly bush. Today, herbal teas are still very popular.

Zz

Z is for Zatar. Zatar is an herb that grows wild in the Middle East. People have been putting it on their bread for thousands of years.

There are zillions of different flavors in the world. What is YOUR favorite?

Artist's Notes

The letters in **boldface** after each description tell you on what other pages that particular herb/spice/flavor is also featured. All of them are shown on the cover. See if you can find them.

Anise The various anise (*Pimpinella anisum*) cookies are the Italian *biscotti* (on the plate) and *pizzeli*, which are round flat cookies baked in a waffle-like iron. The small round cookies in the foreground are German *anisscheiben*. Star anise, which has a similar flavor to anise, isn't part of the anise plant, but is the fruit of the *Illicium verum*, an evergreen tree with white bark. **y**

Basil The root of the word basil is the Greek *basileus*, meaning "king," indicating its importance in the herbal hierarchy. Basil is an essential ingredient in many Italian dishes such as pesto and tomato spaghetti sauce. **h, o, t, y**

Cinnamon Cinnamon continues to be exported from Sri Lanka (formerly Ceylon) and India today, as well as other countries. **g2, j, y**

Dill The name dill derives from the Norse word *dilla*, which means "to lull," and is known to have been used in sleeping potions. It is also the secret ingredient in Fannie Sief's chicken soup. **b, y**

Eucalyptus Many varieties of eucalyptus grow in Australia, where it serves as the primary diet for koala bears. Its medicinal properties are found in cough syrups and drops as well as restorative steam baths to ease flu and colds. My dog, Morgan, wears a eucalyptus collar to repel fleas.

Fennel The flowers and leaves of fennel (in the variety *Foeniculum vulgare*) are used in dyes. Fennel is also supposed to improve one's eyesight. **y**

Garlic Gilroy, California, garlic capital of the world, has a garlic festival every summer. They even serve garlic ice cream and fudge! Large heads of garlic are known as elephant garlic. Dracula is supposedly powerless against garlic, which acts as a blood thinner. **b**

Ginger Ginger root is a common ingredient in the cuisines of China, India, Japan, North Africa, the Caribbean and Southeast Asia. The stairs to the gingerbread house are crystallized ginger. The soft drink is an early bottle of Vernor's Ginger Soda. See the **w** page for pickled ginger served alongside the wasabi with sushi. **b, y**

Herb Garden This herb garden is part of Woodland Herbs in Northport, Michigan. The center part of the garden features plants with edible flowers. The herb garden in the boat is a restaurant herb garden on the island of North Haven off the Maine coast. **y**

Irish Sea Moss *Carraigín* is the Irish Gaelic word for Irish sea moss. Author Jerry Pallotta used to gather the sea moss in Scituate, Massachusetts, by scraping it off the rocks with a rake from his sea dory. On Prince Edward Island, in Canada, the sea moss is thrown onto shore by the surf where people collect it in net cages dragged by horses.

Java Legend has it that an Ethiopian goatherder discovered the stimulating properties of the bean when he found his goats jumping about after eating the berries of the plant. Although many think that "mocha" means "chocolate," it actually is a blend of the Yemen Mocha Mattari and Indonesian Java coffee beans. The green machine is an old-fashioned coffee grinder and the other is an elaborate antique espresso maker from Italy. Cappuccino is a combination of espresso and steamed milk topped off with either cinnamon, nutmeg, or shaved chocolate.

Kola In West Africa, where kola trees are a native plant, Africans have long been chewing kola nuts for their stimulating properties and to sweeten breath. The container is an early Coca-Cola® syrup dispenser used at soda fountains.

Lavender The word lavender comes from the Latin *lavare* which means "to wash." Lavender is used in many bathroom items, including toilet water, soap, lotion, and perfume. The scented lavender wand is a bunch of lavender with its stems turned back and ribbon laced through the stems to contain the leaves and flowers. Dried lavender is also used in sachets and in potpourri, which is an assortment of fragrant herbs set in a bowl to scent a room. Cooks use lavender in cakes, cookies, jams, and flavored vinegar. **h, y**

Mustard Dijon mustard comes from Dijon, France. The yellow fatty substance found in the Chesapeake Bay blue crab is nicknamed "mustard."

Maple Maple sap harvesting was an important part of Chippewa Indian life. The Chippewa na for the month of April is *i ckigami sigegi zis* which means "boiling month." In hot weather the Chippewa dissolved maple sugar in cold water for a refreshing drink. The maple leaf is featu on the Canadian flag.

Nutmeg The substance covering the nutmeg nut is another spice called mace. There are grater especially made for grating nutmeg. Connecticut is known as the "Nutmeg State" because peddlers were notorious for fooling people by selling carved wooden nutmegs to them instea the real thing. In soccer, a ball kicked through an opponent's legs is called a "nutmeg." **j**

Oregano The derivation of the word oregano comes from the Greek *oros ganos*, which means " the mountain." **t, y**

Pepper I knew my salt and pepper shaker collection would come in handy one of these days! **b**

Quinine Quinine powder comes from the bark of the tree *Cinchona pubescens*, native to Centra South America and also known as the "fever bark tree." Once widely used to treat malaria, a tropical disease carried by mosquitoes, today quinine is more often prescribed as an antidote leg cramps.

Rosemary Rosemary is known as the herb of remembrance. Bunches of herbs tied together, cal tussie-mussies, were used to ward off the plague and the bad smells of the Middle Ages. In Victorian times, the nosegays took on a more symbolic purpose, with the herb featured in th middle of the arrangement suggesting the prevailing sentiment. The British folksong, *Scarbo Fair* mentions rosemary: "Are you going to Scarborough Fair? Parsley, Sage, Rosemary, and Thyme. Remember me to one who lives there. She once was a true love of mine." Bees prod rosemary honey. The bread is rosemary foccacia, an Italian flatbread. Rosemary is also used scent perfume. **t, y**

Spearmint There are many varieties of mint. Spearmint and peppermint are often used in confectionery. Peppermint Gibralters were the first candies made in the oldest candy store i United States. Ye Olde Pepper Companie, begun in 1806, is still operating in Salem, Massachusetts. **g2, h, i, y**

Tarragon French tarragon is one of the *fines herbes* used in French cooking. The serpentine association comes from its French name, *estragon*, and Latin, *dracunculus*, a little dragon, ref to its pungent taste.

Uva-Ursi The plant *Arctostaphylos uva-ursi*, which means "bear grape" in Latin, is more common known as "bear berry," or in Algonquin as "kinnikinnick." The Chippewa Indians used all parts the uva-ursi. The berries were cooked with meat to season the broth. They smoked the leaves of uva-ursi, combined with tobacco or red willow, to cure headaches. And the scent of the roots of plant, while being smoked, was known to attract deer during the hunt. The plant is also used as a

Vanilla Vanilla flavor is extracted from the beans of the *Vanilla planifola* orchid. **g2**

Wasabi Wasabi is a condiment often served with sushi and sashimi (raw fish) in Japanese restaurants. It is very hot and its nickname in Japanese is *namida* which means "tears." Wasa comes from the root of the plant and can be bought in powdered (just add water) or paste fo

Xocoatl (Chocolate) Chocolate was much prized by the Aztecs who drank it with spices. Cort the Spanish explorer, tried the drink while visiting the Aztec empire, then took it back to S to introduce the delicious drink to a new populace. BAKER'S® Chocolate Company, found Dorchester, Massachusetts in 1765, was the first chocolate business in the United States. In mid 1800's, women dressed as "La belle chocolatiere," the company's logo, distributed porce cups of BAKER'S® cocoa at food conventions throughout the world. Brown-colored Labra retrievers are called Chocolate Labs. In Hershey, Pennsylvania, the streetlights are shaped l Hershey's Kisses®, and the street names reflect the town's main business. **i, j, s, v**

Yaupon Yaupon tea is made from the leaves of a certain holly (*Ilex vomitoria*) and is a popular wintertime drink in the south. But don't drink too strong a brew, because it will make you s Many herbal teas have long been used as medicinal cures. Try to figure out each of the othe teas on this page.

Zatar Zatar, closely related to thyme, grows wild in the mountains of Lebanon and nearby regi It is added to many middle eastern dishes, like couscous, and mixed with olive oil, ground s and roasted sesame spread on flatbread called *manaeech*.